A New True Book

DESERT BIRDS

By Alice K. Flanagan

Subject Consultant
David E. Willard, Ph.D.
Collection Manager of Birds at the Field Museum
of Natural History, Chicago, Illinois

Children's Press®
A Division of Grolier Publishing
New York   London   Hong Kong   Sydney
Danbury, Connecticut

A mourning dove perched on the limb of a saguaro cactus in the Sonoran Desert

I dedicate this book to those interested in protecting desert birds and their habitats.

Library of Congress Cataloging-in-Publication Data

Flanagan, Alice.
    Desert birds / by Alice Flanagan.
        p. cm. — (A New true book)
        Includes index.
    Summary: Discusses birds that live in a variety of deserts all over the world, including subtropical deserts, cool-coastal deserts, and polar deserts.
    ISBN 0-516-01087-5 (lib. bdg.) – ISBN 0-516-20074-7 (pbk.)
    1. Birds—Juvenile literature. 2. Desert animals—Juvenile literature. [1. Birds. 2. Desert animals.] I. Title.
QL676.2.F615   1996   95-25806
598.29'154—dc20   CIP
                                                          AC

PHOTO CREDITS

Animals, Animals — © Robert Maier, 7 (top), 14 (top); © Johnny Johnson, 7 (bottom), 24 (left), 40 (left), 43 (both photos); © Eyal Bartov, 11; © Bates Littlehales, 13 (top right); © R. H. Armstrong 13 (center); © Mickey Gibson, 14 (bottom left); © Charles Palek, 17 (top); © John Eastcott/Yva Momatiuk, 18; © Joe McDonald, 13 (bottom left), 23; © Arthur Gloor, 27; © Hans and Judy Beste, 28 (bottom left); © M. A. Chappell, 28 (bottom right); © Maresa Pryor, 31 (left); © Richard Day, 37; © Ted Levin, 40 (right); © Ben Osborn, 42 (left)

Jeff Foott Productions — © Jeff Foott, 4, 13 (bottom right)

Valan Photos — © John Cancalosi, cover, 2, 6 (top), 13 (top left), 14 (bottom right), 17 (bottom), 21 (center and bottom), 45; © K. Ghani, 6 (bottom); © Val and Alan Wilkinson, 10; © Jeff Foott, 21 (top), 31 (right); © Joyce Photographics, 24 (right), 42 (right); © W. Hoek, 28 (top); © Aubrey Lang, 33; © Wouterloot-Gregoire, 34

Vantage Art — map, 6-7

COVER: Inca Dove in the Sonoran Desert

Project Editor: Dana Rau
Electronic Composition: Biner Design
Photo Research: Flanagan Publishing Services

CONTENTS

Deserts of the World . . . 5

In Search of Food and Water . . . 9

Surviving the Heat and Cold . . . 16

Breeding Behavior . . . 20

Subtropical Desert Birds . . . 26

Cool-Coastal Desert Birds . . . 32

Cold-Winter Desert Birds . . . 35

Polar Desert Birds . . . 39

Those Amazing Birds! . . . 44

Glossary . . . 46

Index . . . 48

About the Author . . . 48

The roadrunner is the state bird of New Mexico.
It builds its nest in low trees or bushes.

DESERTS OF THE WORLD

Under the hot, desert sun in the southwestern United States, a bird races down a road. It is a roadrunner.

The roadrunner is one of several species of birds that make their home in the dry barren deserts of the world. It lives in the Sonoran Desert, one of the driest regions on earth.

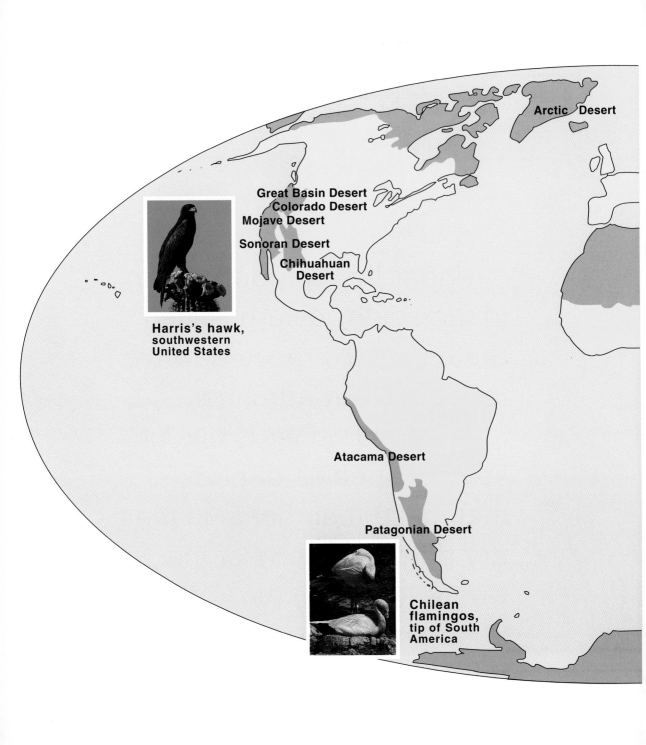

Arctic Desert

Great Basin Desert
Colorado Desert
Mojave Desert

Sonoran Desert

Chihuahuan
Desert

Harris's hawk,
southwestern
United States

Atacama Desert

Patagonian Desert

Chilean
flamingos,
tip of South
America

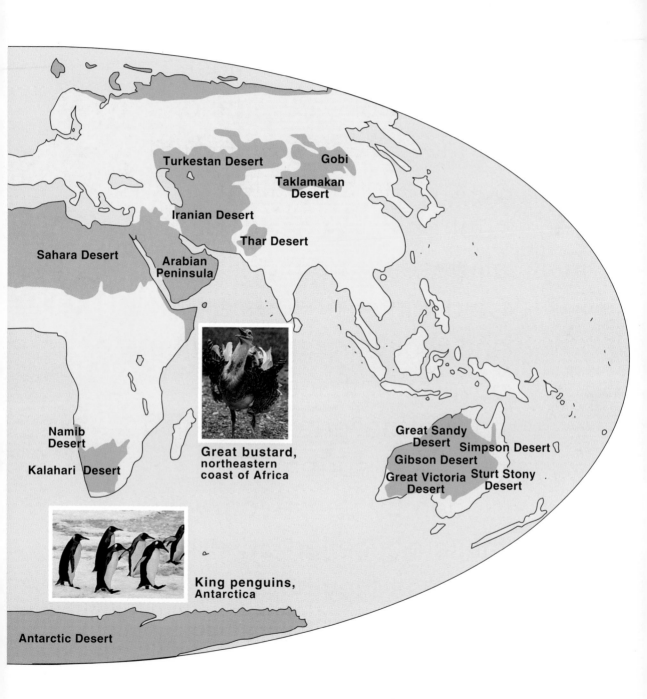

Turkestan Desert

Gobi

Taklamakan
Desert

Iranian Desert

Thar Desert

Sahara Desert

Arabian
Peninsula

Great bustard,
northeastern
coast of Africa

Namib
Desert

Kalahari Desert

Great Sandy
Desert

Simpson Desert

Gibson Desert

Great Victoria
Desert

Sturt Stony
Desert

King penguins,
Antarctica

Antarctic Desert

Deserts cover almost one-third of earth's land surface. Many are hot and sandy and are called subtropical deserts. But not all deserts are hot and dry. Cold-winter deserts are cold and rocky. Polar deserts are covered with ice. Cool-coastal deserts are cooled by ocean currents and hidden by dense fog. All of these are called deserts because they have little or no freshwater available for plants and animals.

IN SEARCH OF FOOD AND WATER

To survive in the desert, birds must find the water they need in drink or in food. Many must go without water for long periods. Some have to travel long distances to reach water.

How much water a bird drinks depends on its size and its needs. Some

Sandgrouse in Algeria

species, such as the trumpeter finch, striped bunting, sandgrouse, and turtledove, drink water on a daily basis. In fact, sandgrouse may travel as far as 50 miles (80 kilometers) daily to reach shores of lakes, where

Pintailed sandgrouse in Israel

they gather in large flocks to drink and bathe. The adult male sandgrouse then carries water back to its young in its thickly feathered breast. At the nest, the young take water from the parent's feathers with their beaks.

Some desert birds can survive without drinking much water. The brown-necked raven, the desert warbler, the ostrich, some chats and bustards, and most larks hardly ever drink. The Gambel's quail and the house finch get most of their water from the buds, grass, and fruit they eat. Birds of prey feed on lizards and other water-filled prey.

Small mammals provide both food and water for birds of prey, such as the Harris's hawk (above left). Some plants also provide food and water. A woodpecker (above right) eats cactus flesh. A hummingbird (center) takes nectar from flowers. Bustards and the Gambel's quail (bottom left and right) eat certain plants.

Arctic terns with fish (above), a
cactus wren with an insect (bottom
left), and a roadrunner with a lizard
(bottom right)

The diets of desert birds vary. What they eat depends on what is available where they live. Birds that live near the ocean, such as coastal birds, polar birds, and cold-winter birds, feed on fish, squid, and krill. In subtropical deserts, some birds prefer to eat leaves, buds, fruits, and seeds. Others eat insects, spiders, and mites. Some even eat snakes, lizards, and small mammals.

SURVIVING THE HEAT AND COLD

In the high temperatures of hot deserts, many birds remain inactive, or dormant, during the day. They rest in the shade of rocks or plants where some spread their wings to cool off. Owls nest in the cactus during the day, and hunt under the cool cover of darkness at night.

(Above) A young horned lark finds shade under a prickly pear cactus.
(Left) A western screech owl cools itself in the hole of a giant saguaro cactus.

17

Other birds spend much of their time flying high above the desert, where the air is cooler. Some birds leave the area, or migrate, during certain times of the year. The cream-colored courser and

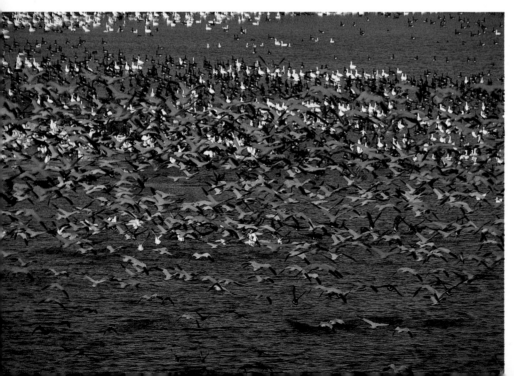

Snow geese in Saskatchewan, Canada, during their fall migration

bar-tailed desert lark leave the northern Sahara at the beginning of spring before the hottest season begins. They travel north, where it is cooler and wetter.

Birds living in cold deserts migrate to warmer and wetter environments before the coldest season begins. Some move to find better conditions during the breeding season. Golden plovers breed in South America and return to the Arctic Circle for summer.

BREEDING BEHAVIOR

At the start of brief but heavy rain in subtropical deserts, birds mate and lay their eggs. The rain also brings new plant and insect growth. By the time the eggs are ready to hatch, food and water are plentiful. When these good conditions are gone, the young birds are ready to survive on their own.

A roadrunner lays from two to nine white eggs.

The Gambel's quail can lay more than a dozen speckled eggs.

In the deserts of Australia, birds nest wherever and whenever they find good conditions. Most species of birds move around a lot. The masked wood swallow often follows the path of rain.

Each September, on the edge of the Patagonian Desert in South America, thousands of Magellanic penguins come to breed. They stay until February, when they and their

A pair of Magellanic penguins in Argentina

offspring return to the
warm waters off Brazil,
1,500 miles (2,414
kilometers) away.

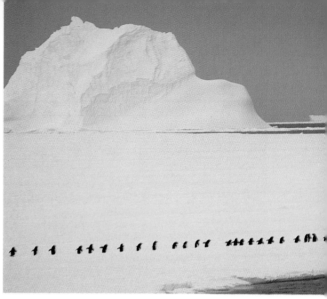

Gentoo penguins in Antarctica
with a brood of chicks (left)
Adélie penguins crossing the
sea ice (above)

In Antarctica, female
emperor penguins lay their
eggs in early winter and
then go off to sea to feed.
The males remain on shore
to protect the eggs during

the winter blizzards. When spring comes, the edge of the sea is teeming with food for the newly hatched chicks.

In open environments of subtropical deserts, birds make nests in bushes and cacti. The desert warbler and the streaked scrub warbler build their nests in bushes. Woodpeckers make holes in the saguaro cactus. After they leave their nests, owls occupy them.

SUBTROPICAL DESERT BIRDS

The Sahara in northern Africa is the largest and hottest of the subtropical deserts. There, the land is always dry. The annual rainfall is only about 4 inches (10 centimeters). Sometimes several years pass without any rain at all.

The Sahara is home to falcons, bustards, hawks, and storks. Finches and

A male and female ostrich in the Kalahari Desert of Africa

sandgrouse live near rocky hillsides and mountains. Numerous larks and wheatears keep cool in the shade. Vultures stay close to oases — or green and wet areas — throughout the desert.

(Left) The sociable weaver builds a nest that may include dozens of smaller nests, each with its own entrance. Large nests may have as many as five hundred birds.

The rainbow bee-eater (bottom left) and the galah parrot (bottom right) are common in Australia.

To the south and east of the Sahara are the Kalahari Desert in Africa and five deserts almost completely covering the continent of Australia. Ostriches are common in the Kalahari Desert. The sociable weaver lives there, too.

A variety of birds live in the Australian deserts. Among the seven hundred or more species are the colorful galah parrot, the green budgerigar, and zebra finches.

In North America, we find the Sonoran, Chihuahuan, and Mojave deserts. In the Mojave, twenty-five species of birds nest in the Joshua tree alone. In the Sonoran, more than twenty species inhabit the saguaro cactus. Others nest in the spiny bushes of the cat's-claw acacia and the mesquite. One of the most interesting birds of the Chihuahuan is the Gambel's quail. It can

The great horned owl (left) and the red-tailed hawk (right) both nest in the Joshua tree.

live its entire life without drinking water, because it gets water from the plants that it eats.

COOL-COASTAL DESERT BIRDS

A few deserts lie along the coasts of South America and Africa. They are called cool-coastal deserts. Here, breezes coming from the cold ocean currents keep the temperature low and the land buried in fog.

On islands near the coast of the Atacama

Desert in Chile, millions of cormorants and pelicans nest. They are well adapted to salt water. Other water birds, including flamingos and ducks, abound in the

Cormorants mate for life and raise their young together.

South American flamingos have pale pink feathers.
Flamingos eat shellfish and small water plants called algae.

salt marshes. The shores
of Africa's Namib Desert
teem with flamingos and
pelicans, too. Inland, there
are ostriches, sandgrouse,
vultures, owls, larks,
buntings, and chats.

COLD-WINTER DESERT BIRDS

Cold-winter deserts in Asia, South America, and in the Great Basin and the Colorado Plateau of the United States are hot in summer and bitter cold in winter. The land is dry because it is either too far inland to receive ocean moisture or near a mountain range that blocks rain from falling.

Among the many species of birds living in the Colorado Plateau of the United States are eagles, hawks, owls, vultures, sage sparrows and thrashers, larks, and quail.

More than 150 species of birds live in the Great Basin. Another 300 visit the area for part of the year. Some birds common to the area are the sage sparrow, sage thrasher, sage grouse, and the poorwill.

Eagles, hawks, vultures, and sandgrouse live in the stony Gobi Desert of China and Mongolia. Birds are scarce in many regions of the Iranian and Turkestan deserts except for

The American kestrel is sometimes called a sparrow hawk. It nests throughout the Americas.

migrating birds. Most birds in the Taklamakan Desert in China live in the Lop Nor region, close to the rivers and trees where they roost.

Many birds that live in the Patagonian Desert year-round are walking birds. The rhea and tinamou both prefer to walk. Patagonia also has sandpipers, flycatchers, and plovers. At its most southern point, Magellanic penguins come to mate and raise their young for part of the year.

POLAR DESERT BIRDS

At the top and bottom of earth are polar deserts. Although they are covered in snow, ice, and water, most freshwater is frozen and not available for most of the year. In the north, temperatures at the Arctic Desert ice cap never get above freezing. In the Arctic zone, temperatures usually

stay below 50 degrees
Fahrenheit (10 degrees
Celsius). Only a few Arctic
birds, such as ptarmigans
and owls, remain in the

A horned puffin (left) and an
artic tern with its chick (right)

tundra during the winter. Their coats turn white and blend in well with the ice and snow.

During the brief summer months, the Arctic tundra becomes a wet marsh. Sandpipers, plovers, swans, geese, and ducks return to feed on the swarms of insects. Along the cliffs of the coast, flocks of puffins abound. And there, the arctic tern returns to breed.

In the Antarctic Desert, temperatures always stay

A wandering albatross (left) nests in the subzero weather of Antarctica. Hungry skuas (right) eat the remains of a fulmar chick.

below freezing. A variety of species live on or around Antarctica during the summer mating season. Albatross, petrels, cormorants, gulls, sheathbills, skuas, and

42

Macaroni penguins
(left) and a lone
king penguin (right)

terns feed on everything from
fish, squid, krill, and penguin
eggs to plants and insects.
Seven species of penguins
breed and raise their young
on huge floating pieces of
ice called ice floes.

THOSE AMAZING BIRDS!

Birds have adapted well to desert life from the South Pole to the North Pole and all the deserts in between. From this amazing group of animals we learn what it takes to survive in some of the harshest conditions on earth.

GLOSSARY

adapt (a-DAPT) — to get used to living a certain way

barren (BAR-uhn) — to have little or no plant life

breast (BREST) — the front part of the body

breed (BREED) — to produce or increase by reproduction

current (KUHR-uhnt) — water moving in a particular direction

desert (DEH-zuhrt) — a region with little or no freshwater

dormant (DOR-ment) — in an inactive state

fog (FAHG) — a mass of water droplets floating in the air near the ground or water

hatch (HACH) — to come forth from an egg

ice floe (ICE FLOW) — a huge floating piece of ice

inhabit (in-HAB-it) — to live in

krill (KRIL) — tiny floating sea creatures

mate (MAYT) — to join as partners; to breed

migrate (MY-grayt) — to move from one country, or place, to another at specific times

mite (MYT) — a tiny, spiderlike animal

moisture (MOYS-chuhr) — the amount of water that makes the air feel wet

nectar (NEHK-tuhr) — a sweet liquid given off by plants

oases (oh-AY-seez) — fertile green spots in deserts

offspring (AWF-spring) — the young of an animal

period (PEER-ee-uhd) — a set amount of time

region (REE-juhn) — a broad geographical area

roost (ROOST) — to settle down for rest or sleep

salt marsh (SAWLT MARSH) — an area of soft, wet land

scarce (SKAYRS) — hard to find

species (SPEE-sheez) — animals that form a distinct group made up of related individuals

teem (TEEM) — to be full of something

INDEX

(**Boldface** page numbers indicate illustrations.)

Albatross, 42, **42**

American kestrels, **37**

Antarctic desert, 24, 41–43, 44

Arctic desert, 19, 39–41, 44

Arctic terns, **14, 40,** 41

Atacama desert, 32–33

Breeding, 19, 20–25, 38

Brown-necked ravens, 12

Buntings, 10, 34

Bustards, **7,** 12, **13,** 26

Cactus wrens, **14**

Chats, 12, 34

Chihuahuan desert, 30

Coastal deserts, 8, 15, 32–34

Cold-winter deserts, 8, 15, 35–38

Colorado Plateau, the, 35, 36

Cormorants, 33, **33,** 42

Cream-colored coursers, 18

Ducks, 33, 41

Eagles, 36

Falcons, 26

Finches, 10, 12, 26, 29

Flamingos, **6,** 33, 34, **34**

Flycatchers, 38

Food gathering, 9–15, 16, 24, 25

Galah parrots, **28,** 29

Gambel's quails, 12, **13, 21,** 30–31

Geese, **18,** 41

Gobi desert, 37

Great Basin, the, 35, 36

Green budgerigars, 29

Gulls, 42

Harris's hawks, **6, 13**

Hawks, **6, 13,** 26, **31,** 36, **37**

Hummingbirds, **13**

Kalahari desert, **27,** 29

King penguins, **7, 43**

Larks, 12, **17,** 19, 27, 34, 36

Magellanic penguins, 22, **23,** 38

Masked wood swallows, 22

Migration, 18–19, 38

Mojave desert, 30

Mourning dove, **2**

Namib desert, 34

Ostriches, 12, **27,** 29, 34

Owls, 16, **17,** 25, **31,** 34, 36, 40–41

Patagonian desert, 22, 38

Pelicans, 33, 34

Penguins, **7,** 22, **23,** 24, **24,** 38, 43, **43**

Petrels, 42

Plovers, 19, 38, 41

Polar deserts, 8, 15, 19, 24–25, 39–43

Poorwills, 36

Ptarmigans, 40–41

Puffins, **40,** 41

Quail, 12, **13, 21,** 30–31, 36

Rainbow bee-eaters, **28**

Rheas, 38

Roadrunners, **4,** 5, **14, 21**

Sage grouse, 36

Sage sparrows, 36

Sage thrashers, 36

Sahara desert, 19, 26, 29

Sandgrouse, 10, **10,** 11, **11,** 27, 34, 37

Sandpipers, 38, 41

Sheathbills, 42

Skuas, 42, **42**

Sociable weavers, **28,** 29

Sonoran desert, **2,** 5, 30

Storks, 26

Subtropical deserts, 8, 15, 20, 25–31

Swans, 41

Taklamakan desert, 38

Tinamou, 38

Turtledoves, 10

Vultures, 27, 34, 36, 37

Warblers, 12, 25

Water, 8, 9–15, 20, 22, 26, 31, 33, 35, 39, 41

Wheatears, 27

Woodpeckers, **13,** 25

ABOUT THE AUTHOR

Alice K. Flanagan is a freelance writer and bird advocate. She considers her strong interest in birds, and a feeling of kinship with them, a symbol of her independence and freedom as a writer. She enjoys writing, especially for children. "The experience of writing," she says, "is like opening a door for a caged bird, knowing you are the bird flying gloriously away."

Ms. Flanagan lives with her husband in Chicago, Illinois, where they take great pleasure in watching their backyard birds.